Good and Bad Germs

by Rod Barkman

Minneapolis, Minnesota

Credits

All images are courtesy of Shutterstock.com, unless otherwise specified. With thanks to Getty Images, Thinkstock Photo, and iStockphoto.
Cover – Svetlana Shamshurina. Recurring – ONYXprj, robuart, Anatolir. 4–5 – MaryDesy, ClassicVector. 6–7 – Artur Plawgo, Dr_Microbe, wildpixel. 8–9 – Irina Romanova. 10–11 – Nadya_Art, RapidEye. 12–13 – SofiaV, Elvetica, AtlasStudio. 14–15 – Bahau. 16–17 – fstop123 20–21 – svtdesign, Jemastock. 22–23 – Daisy Daisy.

Library of Congress Cataloging-in-Publication Data is available at www.loc.gov or upon request from the publisher.

ISBN: 979-8-88916-971-0 (hardcover)
ISBN: 979-8-89232-493-9 (paperback)
ISBN: 979-8-89232-133-4 (ebook)

© 2025 BookLife Publishing
This edition is published by arrangement with BookLife Publishing.

North American adaptations © 2025 Bearport Publishing Company. All rights reserved. No part of this publication may be reproduced in whole or in part, stored in any retrieval system, or transmitted in any form or by any means, electronic, mechanical, photocopying, recording, or otherwise, without written permission from the publisher. Bearport Publishing is a division of Chrysalis Education Group.

For more information, write to Bearport Publishing, 5357 Penn Avenue South, Minneapolis, MN 55419.

Contents

Too Small to See 4
Meet the Germs..............6
Everywhere You Look........8
The Good and the Bad 10
Fabulous Food 12
Gut Goodness................14
Marvelous Medicine 16
Nasty Norovirus.............18
Awful Athlete's Foot 20
Contain It! 22
Glossary 24
Index 24

Too Small to See

Some things around us are teeny-tiny. Just how small can they be? Look at the chart below. Can you read all of it?

Can you read this?

Can you read this?

Can you read this?

Can you read this?

Can you read this?

Which is the smallest sentence you can read?

Germs are even harder to see. That's because they are too small to spot with our eyes alone. But they everywhere.

Meet the Germs

Let's meet three main types of germs.

Hi, I'm a **bacterium** (bak-TEER-ee-uhm). I live in your nose. My bacteria friends and I are good . . . most of the time.

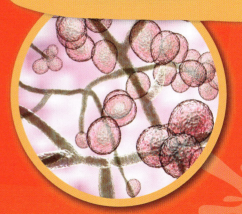

Everywhere You Look

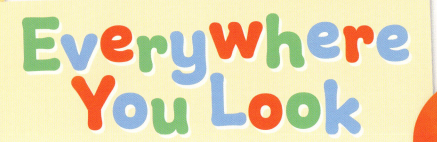

Anywhere you can think of, me and my germ friends are there!

Germs are everywhere. You can't see or feel them, but that doesn't mean they aren't there.

Every **surface** you touch often has germs. Germs can be on the top of tables or desks. They may also get into the air when people cough, sneeze, or even just breathe!

The Good and the Bad

Different germs can do different things to our bodies. Some germs can make us stronger. Others don't **affect** us at all.

See? Most of us are harmless!

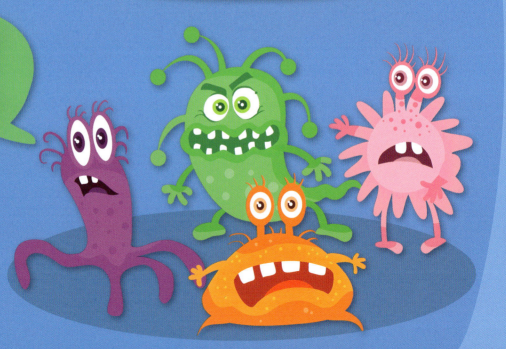

Even so, you might have heard some bad things about germs. That's because some germs can make you sick.

I make your nose runny!

I turn milk into cheese!

Don't eat blue bread!

Fabulous Food

There are many germs found in food. One is called yeast. This is a type of fungus used to help bread dough rise.

Gut Goodness

Germs help the body do its job. Our gut is made up of two parts. There is the **stomach** and the **intestines**. Each has good germs, including bacteria!

Stomach

Intestines

Good gut bacteria helps your body break down the food you eat. These friendly germs turn the food into **nutrients**. They can also fight bad bacteria trying to cause trouble in your body.

Marvelous Medicine

Germs can even help us fight off illnesses. They are in a type of medicine called vaccines (vak-SEENZ). Many vaccines contain a small amount of the germ that could make us sick.

When a doctor gives us a vaccine shot, our bodies learn how to fight those germs. Then, our bodies will remember how to protect us against more of these icky germs in the future.

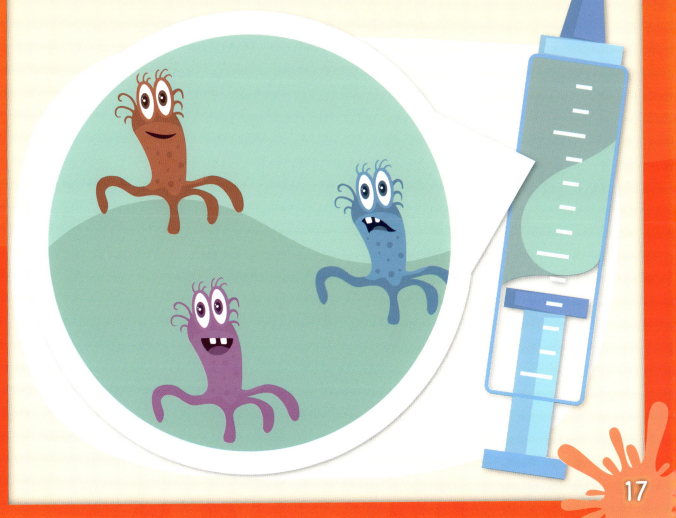

Nasty Norovirus

Bad germs can make us very sick. Different viruses can affect our bodies in different ways. One type of virus that makes us feel very ill is called norovirus (nor-oh-VYE-ruhs).

Norovirus is often called the stomach bug. It can make our stomachs hurt enough that we might throw up or poop. This virus usually makes us sick for a few days when we get it.

I'm warning you! Stay back!

Awful Athlete's Foot

Harmful germs don't just affect the inside of our bodies, they affect the outside, too. Athlete's foot is a foot **infection** caused by a type of fungus.

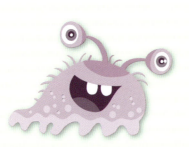

Luckily, athlete's foot is easy to spot. It looks like white patches on the feet. Most often, it pops up between the toes. Your foot might even feel itchy and turn red.

You can treat athlete's foot with a cream from a doctor.

Contain It!

Luckily, there are some ways to stop bad germs from **spreading**.

Cover Your Mouth

Grab a tissue and cover your mouth before you cough or sneeze. This helps stop germs from getting into the air.

Wash Your Hands

Wash your hands in warm water using lots of soap. Clean hands stop germs from spreading when you touch things.

If you stop the bad germs from spreading, you can live safely with good germs.

Glossary

affect to cause something to change

bacterium a tiny living thing that can make you sick or keep you healthy

fungus a plantlike living thing that can't make its own food

intestines the lower part of the digestive system that helps break down food

nutrients things in food that people need in order to grow and be healthy

spreading moving over and covering a bigger distance or area

stomach a part of the body that breaks down the food you eat

surface the outside part or layer of a thing, such as the top of a table

virus a tiny germ that can make our bodies sick

Index

athlete's foot 20–21
bacteria 6, 13–15
food 12, 15
fungus 7, 12, 20
gut 13–15
intestines 14
norovirus 18–19
soap 23
stomach 14, 19
tissues 22
vaccine 16–17
viruses 7, 18–19